WAR
1N
WESTBANK

MIDDLE EAST
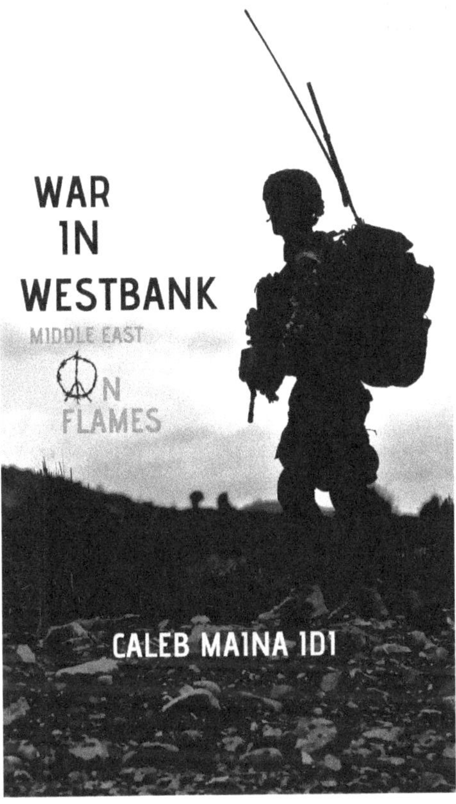

WAR IN THE WEST BANK
MIDDLE EAST ON FLAMES

Table of Contents

- Humanitarian impact of conflicts in the Middle East
- Efforts towards peace and stability in the region

V. Future Prospects

- Potential outcomes of the conflict in the West Bank
- Prospects for stability and peace in the Middle East
- Possible solutions to the conflicts in the region

VI. Conclusion

- Summary of key points
- Implications for the global community
- Call to action for peaceful resolution of conflicts in the Middle East

REFERENCES

The West Bank is a territory located in the Middle East, between Israel and Jordan. The region has been the center of a long-standing conflict between Israel and the Palestinian people. The conflict has its roots in a complex mix of historical, political, and religious factors that have shaped the region over centuries. This conflict has had far-reaching consequences for the people of the region and the international community.

Overview of the Conflict in the West Bank:
The conflict in the West Bank is part of the wider Israeli-Palestinian conflict, which began in the early 20th century with the emergence of Zionist movement and the call for the establishment of a Jewish homeland in Palestine. The conflict intensified in the aftermath of World War II, as Jewish immigration to Palestine increased, and tensions between Jews and Arabs escalated.

In 1948, following the declaration of the State of Israel, Arab countries launched a war against Israel, resulting in the displacement of hundreds of thousands of Palestinians from their homes. The West Bank came under Jordanian control, while the Gaza Strip was administered by Egypt. The conflict continued, and in 1967, Israel captured the West Bank and the Gaza Strip during the Six-Day War.

Since then, the Israeli-Palestinian conflict has been characterized by violence, terrorism, and a lack of progress towards a lasting peace agreement. The West Bank remains a contentious area, with Israeli settlements expanding and Palestinian communities facing restrictions on their movement and access to resources.

Historical Background of the Conflict:

The roots of the conflict in the West Bank can be traced back to the late 19th century, when Zionists began to migrate to Palestine with the aim of establishing a Jewish homeland. This migration intensified after the Balfour Declaration of 1917, in which the British government pledged to support the establishment of a Jewish homeland in Palestine.

The growing Jewish population in Palestine led to tensions with the Arab population, who viewed the migration as a threat to their political and cultural identity. This tension erupted into violence in 1920 and continued throughout the 1930s.

After World War II, the conflict intensified as Jewish immigration to Palestine increased, and tensions between Jews and Arabs escalated. In 1947, the United Nations voted to partition Palestine into separate Jewish and Arab states. The plan was accepted by the Jewish leadership but rejected by the Arab states and the Palestinian Arabs, leading to the 1948 Arab-Israeli War and the displacement of hundreds of thousands of Palestinians.

The West Bank is a strategically important region in the Middle East. It is home to important religious sites, including the Al-Aqsa Mosque in Jerusalem, which is one of the holiest sites in Islam, and the Western Wall, which is one of the holiest sites in Judaism.

The region is also important for its natural resources, including water, minerals, and agricultural land. The Jordan River, which runs through the West Bank, is a major source of water for the region.

The West Bank is also important for its strategic location, situated between Israel and Jordan. Its location has made it a focus of regional and international attention, and its ongoing conflict has contributed to tensions in the wider Middle East.

In conclusion, the conflict in the West Bank is a complex issue with deep roots in history, politics, and religion. The ongoing conflict has had far-reaching consequences for the people of the region and the international community. The importance of the West Bank in the Middle East cannot be overstated, and finding a lasting solution to the conflict remains a crucial challenge for the international community.

The West Bank conflict is a long-standing dispute between Israel and Palestine over the land of the West Bank, a territory in the Middle East that lies between Israel and Jordan. The conflict has its roots in the aftermath of the 1967 Six-Day War, which resulted in Israel's occupation of the West Bank, along with other territories, including the Gaza Strip, the Golan Heights, and the Sinai Peninsula.

Key Players in the Conflict:

The key players in the West Bank conflict are Israel and Palestine. Israel is a Jewish-majority country that was established in 1948 after the end of British rule in Palestine. Palestine, on the other hand, is a predominantly Arab country that was created in 1988, following decades of political struggle against Israeli rule.

Other players in the conflict include the United States, which has historically played a crucial role in mediating the conflict, the United Nations, which has been involved in various peacekeeping efforts, and neighboring Arab countries, which have supported the Palestinian cause.

Timeline of Significant Events:

1948: The State of Israel is established, leading to a mass exodus of Palestinian refugees.

1967: The Six-Day War results in Israel's occupation of the West Bank and other territories.

1979: The Camp David Accords are signed, which lead to the establishment of peace between Israel and Egypt but do not address the West Bank conflict.

1987: The First Intifada, or Palestinian uprising, begins, leading to increased tensions and violence in the West Bank.

1993: The Oslo Accords are signed, which provide a framework for a future Palestinian state but do not resolve key issues, such as Israeli settlements in the West Bank.

2000: The Second Intifada erupts, resulting in increased violence and a deterioration of relations between Israel and Palestine.

2005: Israel withdraws from the Gaza Strip but continues to occupy the West Bank.

2014: The Gaza War erupts, leading to a significant increase in violence between Israel and Hamas.

2018: The Trump administration announces its support for Israel's claim to Jerusalem as its capital, sparking outrage among Palestinians and other Arab countries.

2021: Tensions escalate in the West Bank following a series of violent clashes between Israeli forces and Palestinians, resulting in numerous casualties.

Current State of the Conflict:

The West Bank conflict remains unresolved, with both sides continuing to engage in violent and non-violent struggles for control of the territory. One of the most significant issues at the heart of the conflict is the ongoing construction of Israeli settlements in the West Bank, which the Palestinians see as a violation of their right to self-determination.

Other issues include the status of Jerusalem, which both Israel and Palestine claim as their capital, and the right of return for Palestinian refugees who were displaced during the 1948 war.

In recent years, there have been some attempts at peace negotiations, including the 2019 Bahrain Workshop, which was aimed at promoting economic development in the Palestinian territories. However, these efforts have not led to any significant breakthroughs, and the conflict remains a major source of tension and violence in the region.

Humanitarian Impact of the Conflict:

The West Bank conflict has had a significant humanitarian impact, with both Israelis and Palestinians suffering from the ongoing violence and instability. Palestinian civilians have been killed or injured in clashes with Israeli forces, and many have been displaced from their homes due to the construction of settlements.

Israeli civilians have also been affected by the conflict, with frequent rocket attacks from

Palestinian militants targeting Israeli cities and towns.

The conflict has also had a significant impact on the economy and infrastructure of the Palestinian territories, with restrictions on movement and trade making it difficult for businesses to operate and for Palestinians to access basic goods and services.

Overall, the West Bank conflict remains a major challenge for the world.

The West Bank conflict, also known as the Israeli-Palestinian conflict, is a long-standing dispute over land and sovereignty in the Middle East. The conflict dates back to the late 19th century and has been a source of tension in the region ever since. The West Bank is a territory in the region that has been at the center of the conflict for decades. As a result, many countries and international organizations have been involved in trying to find a solution to the conflict. In this article, we will examine the role of the United Nations and the United States, as well as other international actors, in the West Bank conflict.

Role of the United Nations in West Bank Conflict

The United Nations has been involved in the Israeli-Palestinian conflict since its inception in 1948. The UN has played a key role in trying to find a peaceful resolution to the conflict, and its efforts have been instrumental in shaping the current situation in the West Bank.

The UN has passed numerous resolutions on the West Bank conflict over the years, most notably Resolution 242, which was adopted in 1967 after the Six-Day War. This resolution called for the withdrawal of Israeli forces from territories occupied during the war and for the recognition of the sovereignty and territorial integrity of all states in the region.

The UN has also established several agencies to help Palestinians in the West Bank and Gaza Strip. The United Nations Relief and Works Agency for Palestine Refugees (UNRWA) was established in 1949 to provide assistance to Palestinian refugees. The UN Development Programme (UNDP) and the UN Office for the Coordination of Humanitarian Affairs (OCHA) are also involved in providing aid and support to Palestinians in the West Bank.

The UN has also supported the peace process between Israel and the Palestinians, most notably through the Quartet on the Middle East, which was established in 2002. The Quartet consists of the United Nations, the United States, the European Union, and Russia, and is responsible for mediating peace talks between Israel and the Palestinians.

Position of the United States in West Bank Conflict

The United States has been involved in the Israeli-Palestinian conflict for decades and has played a key role in shaping the current situation in the West Bank. The US has traditionally been a key ally of Israel and has supported its policies in the region.

However, US policy towards the conflict has shifted over the years. In 1978, the US helped broker the Camp David Accords, which resulted in a peace treaty between Israel and Egypt. In the 1990s, the

US played a key role in facilitating the Oslo Accords, which were supposed to lead to a peaceful resolution to the conflict.

In recent years, the US has taken a more hands-off approach to the conflict. In 2017, the Trump administration recognized Jerusalem as the capital of Israel and moved the US embassy from Tel Aviv to Jerusalem. This move was widely criticized by Palestinians and many in the international community, who saw it as a blow to the peace process.

The Biden administration has taken a different approach, stating that it is committed to a two-state solution and has been working to restore aid to the Palestinians. However, the US remains a key ally of Israel and has been criticized by some for not doing enough to pressure Israel to end its occupation of the West Bank.

Many other international actors have been involved
in the West Bank conflict over the years, including
the European Union, Russia, and Arab states.

The European Union has been a key player in the
peace process and has been involved in providing
aid and support to the Palestinians. The EU has also
been critical of Israeli settlements in the West Bank
and has called for a halt to their construction and
removal.

Russia has also been involved in the peace process
and has called for a negotiated settlement to the
conflict. Russia has good relations with both Israel
and the Palestinian Authority and has been
involved in trying to bring the two sides together.

Arab states have also played a role in the West Bank
conflict, particularly in supporting the Palestinians.

The Arab League has been critical of Israeli policies in the region and has called for the establishment of a Palestinian state. In recent years, some Arab states, including the United Arab Emirates and Bahrain, have established diplomatic relations with Israel, a move that was seen as a positive step towards peace in the region.

In addition to these international actors, there have been many non-governmental organizations (NGOs) and civil society groups involved in the West Bank conflict. These groups have been involved in providing aid and support to the Palestinians, as well as advocating for a peaceful resolution to the conflict.

The West Bank conflict is a complex and long-standing dispute that has involved many international actors over the years. The United Nations has played a key role in trying to find a peaceful solution to the conflict, while the United States has traditionally been a key ally of Israel.

Other international actors, including the European Union, Russia, and Arab states, have also been involved in the peace process. Despite these efforts, the conflict remains unresolved, and the situation in the West Bank continues to be a source of tension in the region.

The Middle East region has been in a state of turmoil and unrest for decades, with ongoing conflicts, political instability, and human rights violations. The region is home to various ethnic and religious groups, and geopolitical interests of major powers have fueled the conflicts in the region.

The ongoing conflicts in the Middle East are complex, with various actors involved and multiple causes. Some of the key conflicts in the region include the Syrian Civil War, the Israeli-Palestinian conflict, the Yemeni Civil War, the Iraq War, and the ongoing tensions between Iran and its neighboring countries.

The Syrian Civil War began in 2011, with the government of President Bashar al-Assad facing opposition from various rebel groups seeking his overthrow. The conflict has since escalated into a full-blown civil war, with several foreign powers getting involved, including Russia, Iran, and Turkey. The war has resulted in the displacement of millions of people and the death of hundreds of thousands, with widespread human rights violations and war crimes reported.

The Israeli-Palestinian conflict has been ongoing for decades, with the two sides engaged in a territorial dispute over land in the West Bank and Gaza Strip. The conflict has been marked by violence and sporadic outbreaks of fighting, with both sides accusing the other of human rights violations and terrorism.

The Yemeni Civil War began in 2014, with Houthi rebels taking control of the capital city of Sanaa and ousting the government of President Abdrabbuh Mansur Hadi. The conflict has since escalated into a full-blown civil war, with Saudi Arabia and other Arab countries supporting the Yemeni government and Iran supporting the Houthi rebels. The war has resulted in widespread famine, disease, and displacement, with civilians bearing the brunt of the conflict.

The Iraq War began in 2003, with the United States and its allies invading Iraq and toppling the government of Saddam Hussein. The conflict has resulted in the deaths of hundreds of thousands of people, with sectarian violence and instability continuing in the country to this day.

The ongoing tensions between Iran and its neighboring countries, particularly Saudi Arabia, have also contributed to the instability in the region. The two countries are engaged in a proxy war in Yemen and have been involved in supporting opposing sides in conflicts in Syria and Iraq.

The humanitarian impact of the conflicts in the Middle East has been devastating, with millions of people displaced and in need of assistance. The conflicts have also resulted in widespread human rights violations, including torture, extrajudicial killings, and sexual violence.

Efforts towards peace and stability in the region have been ongoing, with various diplomatic initiatives and peace talks taking place. The United Nations and other international organizations have been involved in efforts to find a solution to the conflicts in the region, but progress has been slow and difficult.

In conclusion, the Middle East remains a region in crisis, with ongoing conflicts, political instability, and human rights violations. The humanitarian impact of the conflicts has been devastating, and efforts towards peace and stability in the region have been challenging. The resolution of the conflicts in the region will require a concerted effort from all parties involved, including the international community, to address the root causes of the conflicts and work towards a sustainable solution.

The conflicts in the Middle East have far-reaching implications for the future prospects of the region. While the situation remains highly volatile, there are several potential outcomes that could shape the future of the Middle East. In this section, we will discuss the potential outcomes of the conflict in the West Bank, prospects for stability and peace in the Middle East, and possible solutions to the conflicts in the region.

Potential Outcomes of the Conflict in the West Bank

The conflict in the West Bank has been a major source of tension between Israel and Palestine for decades. The ongoing Israeli occupation of the West Bank has led to the displacement of Palestinian communities, the construction of illegal settlements, and widespread human rights abuses.

There are several potential outcomes of the conflict in the West Bank, including:

A two-state solution: This solution would involve the establishment of a Palestinian state alongside Israel, with the two states coexisting peacefully. The establishment of a Palestinian state would require the withdrawal of Israeli forces from the West Bank and the dismantling of illegal settlements.

One-state solution: This solution would involve the creation of a single state in which Israelis and Palestinians would share power and resources. This solution would require a major shift in Israeli policy towards the occupation and the recognition of the rights of Palestinians.

Continued conflict: If a peaceful resolution to the conflict is not reached, the conflict could continue to escalate, resulting in further violence and instability in the region.

Prospects for Stability and Peace in the Middle East

The prospects for stability and peace in the Middle East remain uncertain, with ongoing conflicts and geopolitical tensions in the region. However, there are several factors that could contribute to a more stable and peaceful future for the region, including:

Diplomatic initiatives: Diplomatic initiatives and peace talks between conflicting parties could help to reduce tensions and foster greater cooperation and understanding.

Economic development: Greater economic development and investment in the region could help to alleviate poverty and inequality, which are major drivers of conflict.

Political reform: Political reform in countries experiencing political instability could help to address the root causes of conflict and promote greater stability.

Regional cooperation: Greater cooperation and collaboration between countries in the region could help to reduce tensions and foster greater stability.

Possible Solutions to the Conflicts in the Region

There are several possible solutions to the conflicts in the Middle East, including:

Diplomatic initiatives and peace talks: Diplomatic initiatives and peace talks between conflicting parties could help to reduce tensions and promote greater cooperation.

Humanitarian aid: Humanitarian aid and support could help to alleviate the suffering of those affected by the conflicts, including refugees and internally displaced persons.

Political reform: Political reform in countries experiencing political instability could help to address the root causes of conflict and promote greater stability.

Economic development: Greater economic development and investment in the region could help to alleviate poverty and inequality, which are major drivers of conflict.

Conflict resolution mechanisms: The establishment of conflict resolution mechanisms could help to address disputes and prevent violence and instability.

Regional cooperation: Greater cooperation and collaboration between countries in the region could help to reduce tensions and foster greater stability.

In conclusion, the future prospects for the Middle East remain uncertain, with ongoing conflicts, political instability, and human rights violations. The conflict in the West Bank remains a major source of tension between Israel and Palestine, with several potential outcomes. Prospects for stability and peace in the region will require a concerted effort from all parties involved, including the international community, to address the root causes of the conflicts and work towards a sustainable solution. Possible solutions to the conflicts in the region include diplomatic initiatives, humanitarian aid, political reform, economic development, conflict resolution mechanisms, and regional cooperation.

VI. Conclusion

The Middle East has been plagued by conflicts and instability for decades, causing immense suffering to the people living in the region. While the reasons for these conflicts are complex and multifaceted, the underlying causes include political, economic, and social factors that have been exacerbated by external interventions and historical grievances.

Despite the challenges, there are several key points that we can draw from the current situation in the Middle East. Firstly, it is essential to recognize the diversity and complexity of the region, including the rich cultural, linguistic, and religious heritage that characterizes many of its societies. Secondly, it is important to acknowledge the role of external actors in exacerbating conflicts, and to work towards a more inclusive and collaborative approach to regional security and stability. Finally, it is crucial to prioritize the needs and aspirations of the people living in the region, including their basic human rights, economic development, and social inclusion.

The conflicts in the Middle East have far-reaching implications for the global community, ranging from economic instability and energy security to geopolitical tensions and regional security threats. In particular, the rise of violent extremist groups such as ISIS and Al-Qaeda has created significant challenges for international security, requiring coordinated efforts to combat the spread of terrorism and extremism.

Moreover, the ongoing conflicts in the region have created significant humanitarian challenges, including large-scale displacement, food insecurity, and refugee crises. These challenges require a comprehensive and coordinated response from the international community, including humanitarian aid, resettlement programs, and support for conflict resolution and peacebuilding efforts.

In light of the ongoing conflicts and instability in the Middle East, it is essential for the international community to take concerted action towards peaceful resolution of these conflicts. This includes support for political dialogue and reconciliation, economic development and social inclusion, and efforts to address the root causes of conflict and instability in the region.

At the same time, it is crucial to prioritize the needs and aspirations of the people living in the region, including their basic human rights, economic development, and social inclusion. This requires a more inclusive and participatory approach to regional security and stability, one that engages all stakeholders in the search for durable and sustainable solutions to the challenges facing the region.

Ultimately, the road to peace and stability in the Middle East is long and complex, requiring sustained efforts and commitments from all stakeholders. However, with a shared vision and a collaborative approach, it is possible to build a more peaceful, prosperous, and inclusive future for the people of the region.

International Crisis Group. (2021). Middle East and North Africa. https://www.crisisgroup.org/middle-east-north-africa

United Nations Development Programme. (2018). Arab Human Development Report 2016: Youth and the Prospects for Human Development in a Changing Reality. https://www.arabstates.undp.org/content/rbas/en/home/library/human_development/arab-human-development-report-2016.html

Amnesty International. (2021). Middle East and North Africa. https://www.amnesty.org/en/region/middle-east-north-africa/

World Bank. (2020). Middle East and North Africa. https://www.worldbank.org/en/region/mena

United Nations. (2021). Middle East. https://www.un.org/en/sections/where-we-work/middle-east/index.html

Aljazeera. (2021). Middle East. https://www.aljazeera.com/where/middle-east/

International Committee of the Red Cross. (2021). Middle East. https://www.icrc.org/en/where-we-work/middle-east

Carnegie Middle East Center. (2021). Middle East. https://carnegie-mec.org/

The Brookings Institution. (2021). Middle East and North Africa. https://www.brookings.edu/region/middle-east-and-north-africa/

The Middle East Institute. (2021). Middle East. https://www.mei.edu/